Nicki Minaj

young reader's library of pop biographies

Adele

Katy Perry

Lady Gaga

Macklemore

Nicki Minaj

young reader's library of **pop biographies**

Nicki Minaj

C. F. Earl

Young Reader's Library of Pop Biographies: Nicki Minaj

Copyright © 2016 by Village Earth Press, a division of Harding House Publishing. All rights reserved. No part of this publication may be reproduced or transmitted in any form or by any means, electronic or mechanical, including photocopying, recording, taping, or any information storage and retrieval system, without permission from the publisher.

Village Earth Press
Vestal, New York 13850
www.villageearthpress.com

First Printing
9 8 7 6 5 4 3 2 1

Series ISBN (paperback): 978-1-62524-441-3
ISBN (paperback): 978-1-62524-386-7
ebook ISBN: 978-1-62524-142-9
  Library of Congress Control Number: 2014933983

Author: Earl, C. F.

Table of Contents

1. On Top, Looking Back	7
2. Coming Up, Finding Success	17
3. Pop Stardom	27
4. Nicki Today	37
Learn Even More	44
Index	46
About the Author & Picture Credits	48

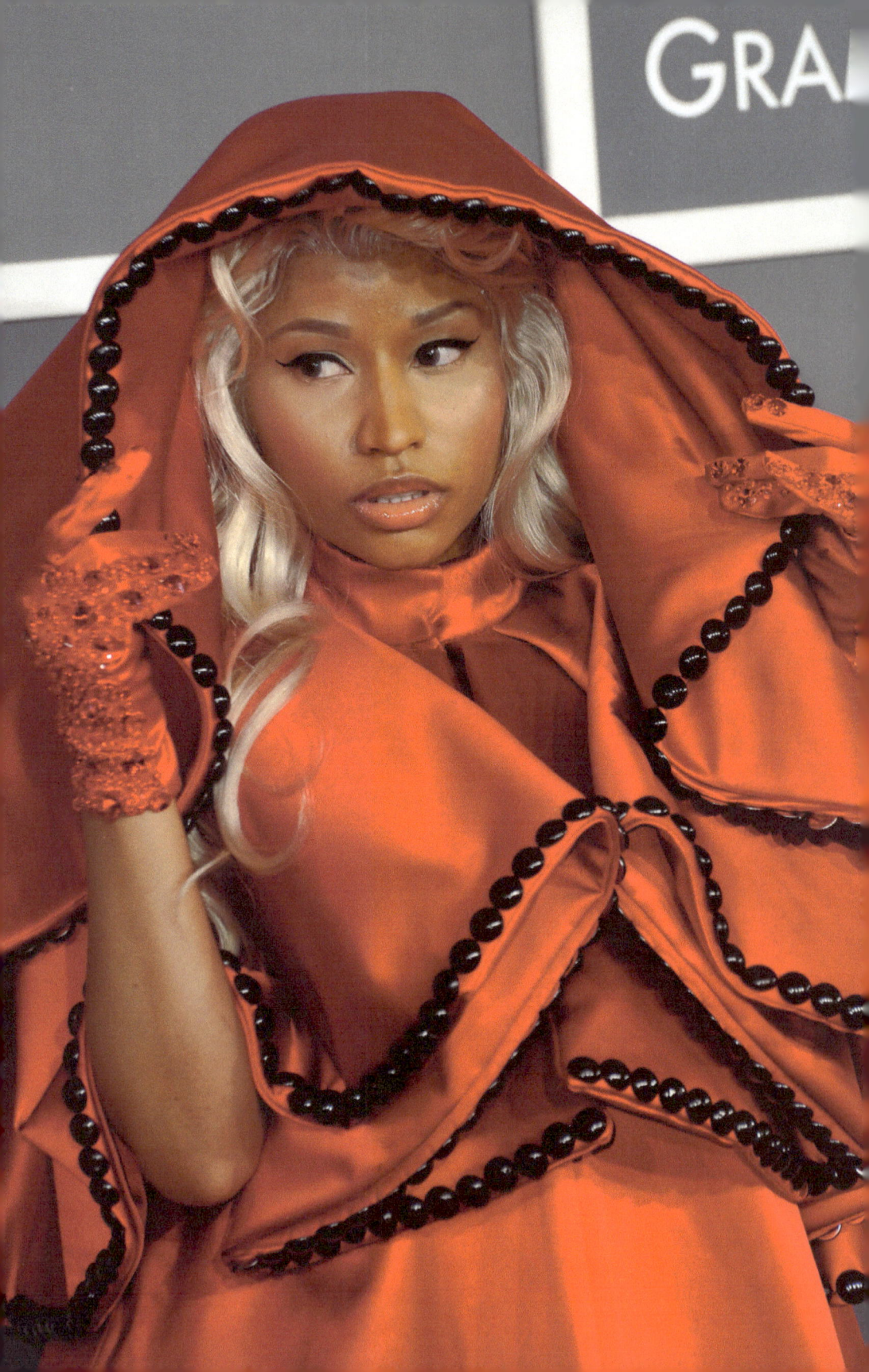

Chapter One

On Top, Looking Back

On a February night in 2012, Nicki Minaj made music history. No other female rapper had ever performed by herself on stage at the Grammy Award show before. Nicki took the Grammy stage to perform "Roman Holiday," a song from her second **album**. Nicki had a come a long way in just a few years. Since 2010, she'd broken records and sold millions of albums. Nicki was a superstar, and performing at the Grammys was proof.

Nicki's performance was like a horror movie, with Nicki as the movie's monster. Nicki pretended to be taken over by a character named Roman. Nicki's fans know the character well. Roman is the dangerous other side of Nicki Minaj. Like many

> An **album** is a collection of songs.

7

other rappers before Nicki, Nicki raps in many different voices. Roman is just one character she plays in her music. On stage at the Grammys, Nicki showed Roman to the world. And many people were shocked by what they saw.

People wrote articles about how strange her costume looked. Some wrote about how odd her voice sounded. Others on **social media** didn't understand her Roman character. Some said her costume was weird. Some wrote that Nicki's performance was scary. But Nicki's true fans loved the performance at the Grammys. They'd heard her rap as Roman before and they understood what Nicki was doing on stage. She was being true to herself and her music.

Many fans had watched Nicki's rise to the top of the music world from the beginning. They loved her first album, *Pink Friday*. They watched her videos and rapped along to her verses. But while many people love Nicki's music, not everyone knows the real Nicki Minaj. She wasn't always the star she is today. Nicki wasn't always as confident and bold as she is now. She had to become the person her fans hear in her songs. Nicki was once just a girl having a hard time with her parents and school like many other kids. Standing on the Grammy stage, making history, Nicki had come a very long way from her hard childhood.

Social media websites like Facebook or Twitter allow people to write to each other and share photos online.

A HARD BEGINNING

Nicki Minaj was born on December 8, 1982. Before she became Nicki Minaj, her name

Music History: The Grammy Awards

The Grammys are one of music's biggest awards. Each year, the Grammys give people in the music business a chance to vote on the year's best music. Presented by the Recording Academy, the Grammys have been around for more than 50 years. The first Grammys were given out in 1959. The first Grammy given to a hip-hop artist was awarded in 1989 to the Fresh Prince (Will Smith) and DJ Jazzy Jeff. Lauryn Hill's album *The Miseducation of Lauryn Hill* was the first hip-hop album to win Album of the Year. When she took the stage to claim her Grammy, she said "This is crazy. This is hip-hop!" For more information about the Grammy Awards, visit www.grammy.com.

was Onika Tanya Maraj. She was born in Trinidad and Tobago, in a town called St. James. St. James is outside the city of Port of Spain.

Nicki's mother, Carol, married Nicki's father, Robert Maraj, when she was twenty years old. Robert was a jealous husband to Carol. He got angry with her often and was mean when he thought she was paying attention to other men. Carol told *Trinidad Express* that Robert would get angry with her for even looking at another man. "If someone who knew me saw me out in the street and I spoke to that person it was a big argument . . . I didn't [realize] it then, those early signs of abuse," she said. "I was very young when the abuse started."

Carol and Robert had children, including Onika. Carol worked a few different jobs in banking and insurance. Robert

New York was very different from Trinidad and Tobago, but Nicki's life in her new city would stay with her as she grew up.

didn't treat her any better, but she felt like she was making a life for herself. When she was twenty-four, Carol moved to New York. She left her children with her mother in St. James. "They were in very good hands," Carol told *Trinidad Express*. "My mom took good care of them."

Carol moved to the Bronx, a borough of New York, and began going to classes at Munroe College. Six months later, Robert came to the United States, too. He moved in with Carol in the Bronx. At first, he was treating Carol much better than he

had before. He promised things would be different. He said he had changed. Carol was happy to have Robert making her dinner and trying to make their marriage better. She also wanted her children to come to New York. She hoped Robert would be a good father in their new home country. Robert got a job at American Express and the couple's children came to the United States a few years later.

Before Nicki moved to New York, Carol got help from her father to buy a new house in Queens. The family moved into a house on 147th Street. It seemed as though life was getting better for the young family, but it was about to take a turn for the worse.

LIVING IN QUEENS

Near the end of 1987, Robert burst into the house angry and yelling. He said he needed money from Carol. But Carol didn't have any money to give him. She didn't understand until then that her husband was addicted to drugs. "There was a lot happening in that house. I didn't know my husband was a crack addict," Carol told *Trinidad Express*.

Carol says that Robert had a terrible childhood. His father died when he was a young teenager. Carol says he had to raise his five brothers and sisters, and that his mother hit him. Carol believes all this may have led to Robert becoming abusive himself. Because of drugs, Robert's abuse became worse and worse.

Carol was scared.

"How did all of this happen?" Carol asked herself. "I was a twenty-seven-year-old woman, working hard, trying to be happy in my own way and then this . . . just comes upon me.

The [neighbors] are hearing. You have to hide your face and bend your head."

Nicki's life was very hard growing up in Robert and Carol's house. Nicki says that her father would hurt her mom when he used drugs or drank alcohol. Once, he even set the family's house on fire. Nicki believed that Robert was trying to kill Carol. "She got out before [the house] burned all the way down," Nicki said.

Nicki also said she had to move schools a lot because her parents always fought. She had to make new friends at each new school, and she hated it. "I had butterflies in my stomach each time," Nicki told *Teen Vogue*. "Are people going to like or hate me? Will they talk about me?"

Nicki's tough life forced her to be strong. With so many changes, Nicki had to learn to believe in herself. When no one else seemed to have confidence in Nicki, she still knew she was special.

Nicki told *Teen Vogue* that she felt other people didn't like her confidence. "I encountered jealous girls a lot—it wasn't like I had nice clothes, so they couldn't be envious of that, but they were like, 'You shouldn't be that confident.'"

Nicki also faced bullies at school—but she didn't lose her belief in herself. "I let people know I wasn't going to be pushed around," Nicki said. "What it came down to is that the bullies wanted me to bow down to them. And I just wouldn't."

Nicki saw her mother being pushed around at home. She didn't want that for herself. Nicki told Details.com that one of the things that pushed her to go into music was her desire to change her mother's life. "I wanted my mother to be stronger, and she couldn't be," Nicki said. "I thought, 'If I'm successful, I can change her life.'"

Life was hard at home, but Nicki got good grades at school. She did a lot of activities outside of school to keep herself busy, including playing the clarinet in middle school. Soon, Nicki was heading into high school.

FINDING HER VOICE

Nicki went to Fiorello H. LaGuardia High School in New York City. LaGuardia isn't a regular high school. At LaGuardia High School, students study acting, music, and performing. They work on plays and playing instruments. They study singing and dance. Nicki loved acting. At first, she thought she might sing at the school, but she ended up sticking to the stage.

"It was the first time I felt like I really fit in," Nicki told *Teen Vogue*. "Everyone there was creative. For once, I didn't feel like there was something weird about me."

Nicki graduated high school and worked at a few different jobs. She wanted to become an actress in Broadway shows. But things weren't working out for her at first. Nicki worked as a waitress at Red Lobster and a few office jobs. While she was looking for work as an actor, she also started rapping. She joined a group called the Hoodstars.

The group broke up, but Nicki started taking rap more seriously. Soon, she had big dreams of making it in the rap world on her own. Nicki always loved performing. And soon, she'd be performing in front of the whole world.

Find Out Even More

Books are a great way of finding out about the lives of your favorite music stars—but one book can never hold all the information you'd want to know about a subject. The author had to pick and choose which facts to put in the book and what to leave out. To see the whole picture, you'll have to read more than one book.

The library is one of the best places to find new books about the things you love. Your school or hometown will probably have a library where you can find a lot of books about hip-hop and music superstars. Finding books at the library is easy if you use the library's catalog. If you have trouble finding a book you want to read, ask a librarian for help.

Try finding some of the books below:

Hatch, Thomas. *A History of Hip-Hop: The Roots of Rap*. Mankato, Minn.: Red Bricklearning, 2005.

Garofoli, Wendy. *Hip-Hop History (Hip-Hop World)*. Mankato, Minn.: Capstone Press, 2010

Gaines, Ann Graham and Reggie Majors. *The Hip-Hop Scene: The Stars, the Fans, the Music*. Berkeley Heights, N.J.: Enslow Publishers, 2009.

Look over the books you've found. Check out the table of contents. Flip to a chapter that seems interesting to you and read over a few pages. As you flip through the pages of these books, ask yourself a few questions:

1. How is the book organized? Is it easy to find information you're looking for? Try using the book's table of contents and index to find a subject that interests you.
2. Does the book have pictures? Do they help you understand the book's subject?
3. Do you have any trouble understanding the book? Not every book is meant for every reader. Some books are written for older readers. Some books are written for people just learning to read. Look for books that match your reading level. Remember to challenge yourself—you don't want a book that's too easy for you. But finding the right book for you is a big part of becoming a better reader.
4. Do you like the book? Would you read more of it? Why or why not? What interests you in the book? Is there information in the book you can't find in another book?

Chapter Two

Coming Up, Finding Success

Nicki started at the bottom of the rap game. She didn't have a big **record label** to sell her music for her. Instead, she had to start her music career like many other new artists by putting her music online for free. She posted music on the social media website MySpace. Nicki hoped getting her music on the Internet would show people how talented she was. She also got a manager to help her get her music out into the world. Meanwhile, she sent her music to people at record companies. Nicki was working hard to break into the music world.

> A **record label** is a company that pays to record music and helps artists to sell their music in stores.

STARTING OUT

In 2007, a man named Fendi saw saw Nicki's MySpace page. Fendi worked as the head of the Dirty Money Records, an **independent** music company. He listened to some of Nicki's music and knew she could be a star. Later that year, he helped her put out her first **mixtape**, *Playtime Is Over*.

After *Playtime Is Over*, Nicki released a mixtape called *Sucka Free* in 2008. Fendi also filmed a short talk with Nicki for a DVD. The DVD was part of *The Come Up* series.

More and more people started to take notice of Nicki's music. They heard it online and shared it with their friends. Soon, Nicki was gaining true fans.

In 2009, Nicki put out her third mixtape. She called the tape *Beam Me Up Scotty*. On the cover, Nicki dressed as Wonder Woman. The bold superhero costume said everything new fans needed to know about Nicki's music.

Nicki told MTV.com that before *Beam Me Up Scotty*, people didn't take her seriously as a rapper. She also said that she wasn't taking her own music as seriously. "I was OK, but I wasn't focusing on the music," she said. "I was doing pictures and stuff like that, so people knew me more for pictures than my music. . . . But with the *Beam Me Up Scotty* mixtape, they have to take me seriously as an artist. So, I would say maybe a year ago, I started sharpening my skills."

> If a music company is **independent**, it isn't one of the major companies in the music business.
>
> A **mixtape** is a group of songs put out for free.

18 NICKI MINAJ

Music History: Rap and the Internet

The Internet has changed the way new rap artists like Nicki become stars. Before the Internet, rappers had to get people in their own city to listen to a CD or cassette tape. Often, artists just starting out had to hand people their music themselves. Many people heard new music through the radio. But most new artists didn't have a chance to be heard.

Today, if artists want people to hear their music, they go to the Internet. And most people find new music online. Now, a rapper from Cleveland can be heard by a rap fan in South Africa. And that fan can share it with his friends in Japan on Twitter.

It's never been easier for new artists to post their music online. But that means there is a lot of competition to be heard on the Internet. Many rappers start by giving away mixtapes of their music online for free. That way, people don't have to spend any money to see if they like a new artist. Free mixtapes given away online are a great way for a new artist to show people their music. Mixtapes have helped rappers like Lil Wayne, Drake, and Nicki become huge stars.

With *Beam Me Up Scotty*, Nicki was gaining even more fans. Music fans began talking more and more about how Nicki was on her way to success. With more people taking notice, Nicki was ready to show the world what she could do with a big company behind her.

With *Pink Friday*, Nicki was headed for stardom, but first she'd have to break into the music business.

NICKI'S BIG BREAK

In August 2009, Nicki signed a **record deal** with Young Money Entertainment. Young Money is rapper Lil Wayne's label. He'd

A **record deal** is an agreement between an artist and a record label for the label to sell the artist's music.

seen Nicki on *The Come Up* DVD in 2008. After hearing her music, he knew she could be rap's next big star. A year later, she was signing a deal with his company. Now, she had a company with the power to get her music to more people than ever.

In 2009, Nicki recorded music with many different artists. She worked with singer Robin Thicke, and she worked with rapper Yo Gotti. With each verse she rapped on someone else's song, she became more popular. Soon, she would be working with some of the biggest stars in music.

At the end of the year, Young Money Entertainment released an album called *We Are Young Money*. The album showed off the company's rappers, including new stars Drake and Nicki. One song on the album, "Bedrock," became a hit in the United States and the UK. The song made it to number 2 on the *Billboard* Hot 100 chart in the United States.

In 2010, Nicki seemed to be everywhere. She had an amazing year and became one of the most exciting artists in music. She rapped verses on songs by artists Mariah Carey, Kanye West, and Drake. In January, she worked with Carey on the song "Up Out My Face." Later in the year she recorded a popular verse on Kanye's song "Monster." Nicki also performed on stage with some of hip-hop's other biggest names.

Nicki talked to *Interview Magazine* about how she felt about some of her favorite moments of the year. "One of the biggest highlights of this year was being onstage with Jeezy, Wayne, and Drake in the middle of Jay-Z's set at Madison Square Garden," Nicki told the magazine. "[I] was in a video with Mariah Carey! I still haven't gotten over that!"

Nicki also told *Teen Vogue* that recording "Monster" was a great moment for her. "[Never] in a million years did I think I'd

Music History: The *Billboard* Charts

Billboard magazine started in 1894. At first, the magazine showed people where they could find entertainment. Later, the magazine focused more on music. In the 1930s and '40s, *Billboard* started tracking which music was most popular. Each kind of music had its own chart in the magazine, with the most popular music reaching the top spot for its chart. For decades, getting a number-one song on the *Billboard* charts has been a sign of success for artists and music companies.

get a chance to record a song with Jay-Z or to be on a Kanye West album," she said.

After an amazing year, Nicki decided to end it with a bang. She was ready to release her own music. At the end of 2010, Nicki released her first album, *Pink Friday*.

NICKI'S PINK FRIDAY

Nicki had been working on her first real album for a long time. She had even saved out songs for the album while she was working on her mixtape *Beam Me Up Scotty* back in 2009. Nicki told *XXL Magazine* that the songs were "too good to put on a mixtape."

"Very soon we'll start releasing stuff," she told the hip-hop magazine.

Before the album came out, Young Money president Mack Maine predicted that Nicki's new album would do very well.

He said that Nicki had found her own place in the music world. "Nicki can sing, rap, she just giving you what she feel like giving you," Mack told *Vibe Magazine*. "When you doing you, it's nothing you can mess up at because you're being yourself. She's found herself, she's found her lane, so there's not really too much to be nervous about."

Nicki had worked with some big names on her first album. She had a song with rapper Eminem called "Roman's Revenge." The song introduced Nicki's new fans to her character Roman. Nicki also recorded songs with Rihanna and Drake for *Pink Friday*.

Pink Friday came out on November 19, 2010, and it was a huge success. In just one month, *Pink Friday* sold a million copies. Soon, people around the country were rapping along with Nicki's verses and singing her songs. Country singer Taylor Swift rapped her verse from "Super Bass" in a radio interview. Actress Michelle Trachtenberg rapped the same verse in a YouTube video.

In 2011, Ellen DeGeneres had two little girls from England rap "Super Bass" on her television talk show. Sophia Grace was eight years old and her cousin was only five. But the two were already Nicki Minaj fans.

Nicki's song "Super Bass" became a huge hit, reaching number ten on the *Billboard* pop song charts. Nicki was becoming a huge star. After starting from the bottom, Nicki was on top of the rap game.

Find Out Even More

Reading books is one of the best ways to learn more about the things you love. But books aren't the only place to find fun facts about music stars or the music business. A book can only hold so much information, but the Internet has no limits!

Online, though, you have to search for information yourself—there is no author to put the facts together for you. But there is much more information online than could ever be held in a single book. If you've read books about a subject and still want to know more, the Internet is the best place to look.

Using search engines helps to narrow down all of the information on the Internet. Search engines like Google, Bing, or Yahoo find websites for you based on keywords. Type a few words into the search bar on Google.com, and you'll find millions of websites about that topic. Make sure you pick your keywords carefully. The wrong keywords can lead you far from information you're interested in.

The Internet is also a good place to get more information about things that are mentioned in a book but not explained in detail. To find out more details connected with Nicki's story, try searching for some of the keywords below:

Trinidad and Tobago
The Grammys
Lil Wayne
hip-hop

Chapter Three

Pop Stardom

At the 2012 Grammys, Nicki was **nominated** for three awards: she was nominated for Best New Artist; *Pink Friday* was nominated for Best Rap Album; and her song with Drake, "Moment 4 Life," was nominated for Best Rap Performance. Nicki didn't win any Grammys, but she did get to perform her song "Roman Holiday," making history. Even without a Grammy, Nicki had already become one of the most successful rap artists in music.

After the success of Nicki's first album, she was quick to come back with more music in 2012. In April of that year, Nicki released *Pink Friday: Roman Reloaded*. She

> When someone is **nominated**, they are chosen to be part of a group competing for an award.

Nicki is never just one thing. She can be sweet and tough. She can be glamorous or wild. Her music is pop and hip-hop. Different fans like different sides of the creative rap star.

28   NICKI MINAJ

had already become a star, but with her second album, Nicki was ready to get even bigger.

NICKI RELOADED

Nicki's second album was another huge success. On *Roman Reloaded*, Nicki pushed her music in new directions. With the song "Starships," Nicki showed new fans that she could sing on a song with very little rapping. With "Beez in the Trap," she also proved she could rap with the best artists in hip-hop. Many of Nicki's lyrics focused on her wild character Roman. But other lyrics were tender and showed her softer side. No matter which part of herself she showed in her songs, fans loved Nicki's new music.

Like *Pink Friday* before it, *Roman Reloaded* was a hit. In its first week out, the album hit number one on the *Billboard* album charts. *Roman Reloaded* sold more than 250,000 copies in that week alone. "Starships" became a hit, reaching number five on the *Billboard's* pop song chart. The song's pop sound helped Nicki gain new fans. "Super Bass" had gotten many people to take notice of Nicki, but "Starships" was an even bigger hit.

Not every Nicki Minaj fan loved the rapper's pop sound, though. Some hip-hop fans wanted Nicki to go back to the way she'd rapped when she first started becoming famous. Still, Nicki was bigger than ever after *Roman Reloaded*'s release.

After putting out her second album, Nicki was ready to tour the world. Now she would rap for her fans around the globe. The Pink Friday Tour started in the spring of 2012. Nicki performed across North America, Europe, and Asia.

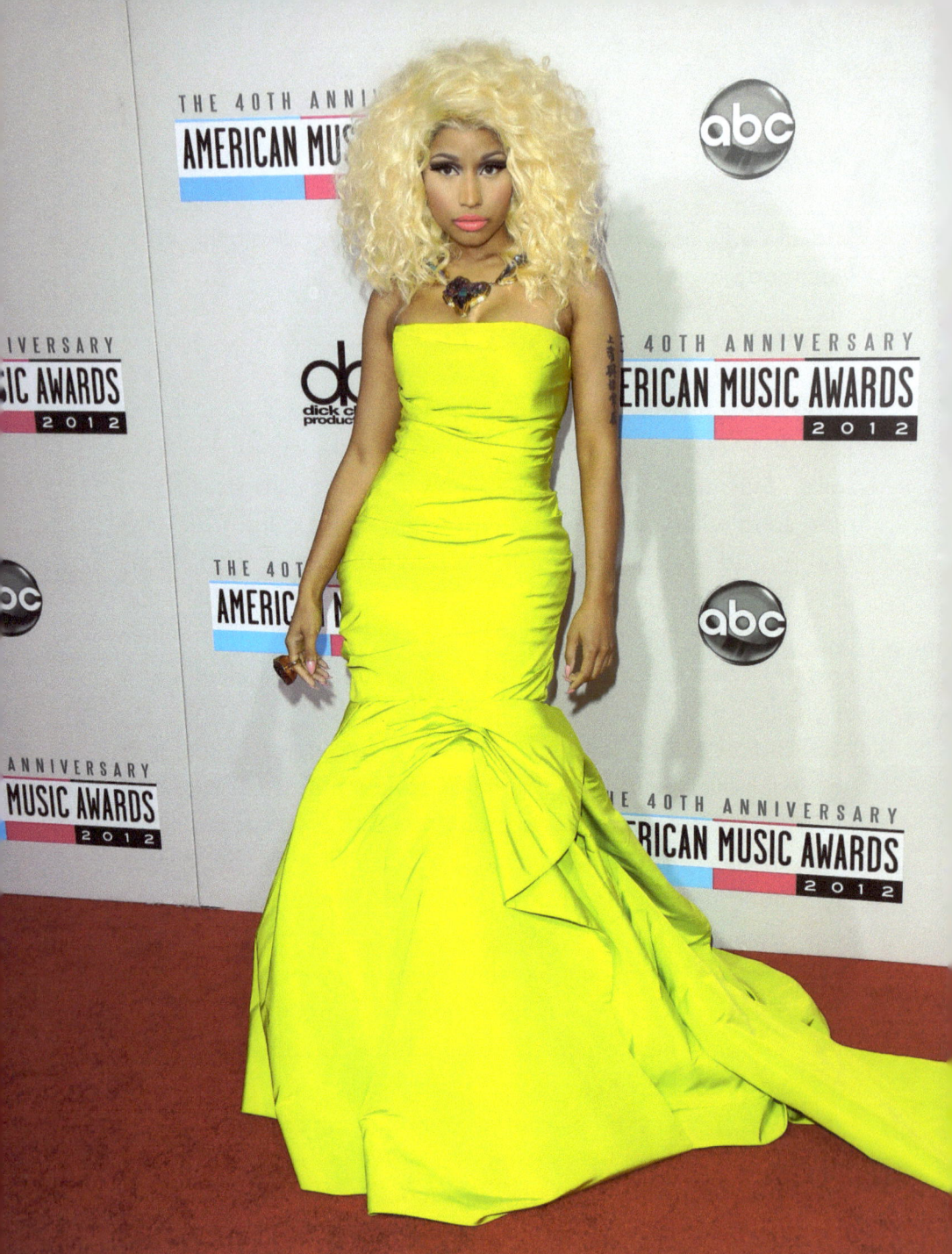

After releasing her second album, Nicki had become one of the most famous women in music. Soon, she'd have new opportunities to branch out and do even more.

Music History: Gold and Platinum Albums

The Recording Industry Association of America (RIAA) has been awarding artists with gold and platinum records for years. The RIAA gives gold records to artists for 500,000 records sold, and platinum records for one million sold. The RIAA has been giving awards for music artists since 1958, but the awards have changed over the years. At first, the awards were given based on the amount of money a song or album made instead of the number of sales. The RIAA's first award was gold, and then the platinum award was added in 1976. For more information about the RIAA's awards for artists, visit RIAA.com.

NICKI MINAJ: AN AMERICAN IDOL

Soon, Nicki was ready to take on a new challenge. In September 2012, Nicki was named one of the new judges on *American Idol*. She would step in as a judge for the singing competition's twelfth season. Country singer Keith Urban and pop star Mariah Carey joined Nicki as new judges on the show. Nicki said she was ready to help.

Long-time Idol judge Randy Jackson was excited to have Nicki be part of the show. When she was chosen as a new judge, he said, "[Nicki] brings a whole other cool vibe we've never had on the show."

Nicki's time on Idol wasn't always easy. She had a tough time getting along with Mariah Carey. The two fought on the show and sometimes on Twitter. Nicki worked on the show for

Being chosen to judge *American Idol* was a big deal for Nicki. She'd become a big enough star to coach other artists on making it in the music world.

just one season. In October 2013, the show announced that both Nicki and Mariah were moving on. Nicki told her fans on Twitter that she was leaving *Idol* by thanking the show: "Thank you *American Idol* for a life changing experience! Wouldn't trade it for the world! Time to focus on the Music!!! Mmmuuuaahhh!"

Fox, the television network that puts on *American Idol*, thanked Nicki for her time at the show as well. The company

Nicki didn't always get along with Mariah Carey, but the fights between the judges made for interesting television!

wrote in a statement that Nicki "brought a level of honesty and passion to *American Idol*."

    Some reports say Nicki made more than $10 million for her time on the twelfth season of *Idol*. Her time there is proof that she's one of music's biggest stars.

Pop Stardom

Find Out Even More

Try searching for Nicki Minaj on Google.com and you'll find millions of websites about Nicki. Check out some of the results from the first page of Google search results below:

Nicki Minaj

mypinkfriday.com

Nicki Minaj—Wikipedia, the free encyclopedia

en.wikipedia.org/wiki/Nicki_Minaj

IG: @NickiMinaj (NICKIMINAJ) on Twitter

twitter.com/NICKIMINAJ

Nicki Minaj | New Music And Songs | MTV

www.mtv.com/artists/nicki-minaj

Nicki Minaj —YouTube

www.youtube.com/artist/nicki-minaj

Nicki Minaj News, Pictures, and Videos | TMZ.com

www.tmz.com › Celebs

And that's just a few results out of the millions Google can find online. Not every site is a good source of information about Nicki, though. Which of the sites above is your best choice if you want to learn more about Nicki?

MyPinkFriday.com is Nicki's official site, so it's probably the best place to find all the latest information about Nicki's music and her businesses. Nicki also uses social media sites like Twitter. On Twitter, you can be sure you're hearing from Nicki herself because of the blue checkmark on her Twitter page. Nicki has a "verified" account on the site, which means Twitter has checked to make sure it's really Nicki. Social media sites are good for hearing from artists, but they aren't always good sources of information. Sometimes, social media is more about what people think than what is true.

Fan websites are another source of information about music artists. These sites are run by people who love the artist, but not the artist themselves. Fan sites can be a lot of fun, but they aren't perfect. They can post information that may or may not be true because the fans post the information themselves. Wikipedia pages for artists also have information posted by fans. Make sure to check for the numbers that appear after some of the facts on Wikipedia. Clicking on the small number can lead you to the website where that information was first posted. Checking facts on Wikipedia is important when you're searching for true information about your favorite artists.

Chapter Four

Nicki Today

Nicki is one of the most successful women in music today. But she's not just successful in music. She's also made her name in fashion, business, and television. Nicki's style has made her an **icon**. People look to see what Nicki's wearing because it will always be something to talk about. Now, Nicki is turning her style into her own businesses and brands.

NICKI'S BUSINESS

Nicki has worked with makeup company MAC Cosmetics on lipstick. In 2010, Nicki and MAC put out "Pink 4 Friday" just in time for the launch of her first album.

An **icon** is someone other people look up to.

Nicki also has her own perfumes. One is called Pink Friday, and the other is called Minajesty. Each bottle is shaped like Nicki herself, each wearing a different outfit and hairstyle.

Nicki's even going to selling her own clothing at Target, Walmart, and other stores. She's calling her clothing the Nicki Minaj Collection.

Nicki's worked in commercials, too. She has been in a Pepsi advertisement and a commercial for Adidas. She's also worked in commercials for Dr. Dre's Beats headphones.

Nicki has started to talk about forming her own record label. The company doesn't have a name yet, but Nicki is sure to take over the business side of music just as she's taken over the radio and pop charts. Nicki is more than an artist. She's a talented businessperson.

LOOKING TO THE FUTURE

Today, Nicki is working on new music. Fans are excited to hear Nicki's third album and she doesn't want to disappoint them. She's said she wants to get back to her roots as a rapper on her new album. She told New York radio station Hot 97 that she wants to make music for fans of hip-hop. She wants to do something different from the pop music of her second album.

"If I really wanted to, I could go back in and make another pop song like ['Starships'] to sell but I'm choosing not to do it," she told the station. "I'm choosing to get back to my **essence** and feed the core hip-hop fan."

Along with working on new music, Nicki's also branching out into

> A person's **essence** is what make that person who she is.

Nicki's Barbies

Nicki has a close bond with her fans. She calls her fans "Barbies" or "Barbz" for short. She is always quick to thank her fans and let them know what they mean to her. She told *Teen Vogue* she even feels like her fans are as close to her as family.

"[My fans] feel like my little sisters and brothers," Nicki said. "I have this urge to protect them and have fun with them at the same time."

Online, at concerts, and in interviews, Nicki is always talking about her Barbies. And now Nicki has her own Barbie! After years of Nicki calling her fans "Barbies," toy company Mattel made a Nicki Minaj Barbie. The special doll was sold for charity for thousands of dollars. Nicki told Billboard.com that it was an important moment for her.

"It's just a one of a kind. . . . I never thought Mattel would even pay attention to me," she said. "For me this is a very major moment, because it just shows that you can come from nothing and still be a force in the main world, a business woman, and hopefully a mogul one day."

acting. She was in a movie starring Cameron Diaz called *The Other Woman*, released in April, 2014. Nicki also recorded a voice for 2012's *Ice Age: Continental Drift*, an animated movie. Nicki's high school dream of acting is finally coming true!

Nicki has done so many amazing things in just a few years, it's hard to say what's next for rap's most successful woman. One thing is for sure, Nicki will always be herself. She doesn't care that people think she's strange.

Nicki's never been afraid to dress and act the way she wants, even if other people think she's strange or silly.

She told *Interview Magazine* that she doesn't mind if people call her "a weirdo." "There are a lot of people in hip-hop who are probably never going to get what I do," Nicki said. "But, by just being myself, I end up touching a lot more people who might never have paid much attention to a female rapper."

Nicki told *Teen Vogue* that she doesn't pay attention to people who say nasty things about her. "I used to read the bad things people said about me," she said. "Then I asked myself, 'Why am I reading that when I have millions of people saying great things?' You cannot give negativity power. I tell teens, if you're having a problem, there's nothing wrong with deleting your social media. If people keep taunting you and you keep reading it, it's poison."

Nicki's always found confidence in herself. In her music, she plays fierce characters like Roman. She speaks her mind with confidence. With her special style, Nicki has never been afraid of what other people might think of her. She wears what she wants in the same way she says what she wants.

Nicki is beginning to work more in movies and she'll be releasing new music soon. Nicki's next big idea is a secret only she knows today, but fans watch for every bit of news. No matter what she does on her next album—pop or hip-hop, rapping or singing—it's likely to be a huge success.

Nicki has already proven that she can sell more records than most music artists. She's building businesses and acting in movies. Nicki's at the top of her game, with more people watching her than ever. Whatever she does next, her fans will be listening and watching. Few stars are bigger than Nicki Minaj!

Find Out Even More

In the same way different books are written for different readers, each website online is different. People make different websites for many different reasons. Knowing who made the website and why they made it is important when looking for information online. To choose the websites that are most useful and interesting to you, you'll need to ask yourself a few questions about each website you visit online:

1. Who made the website? Check for a logo or an "About Us" page on the website to find out more about who runs the site. Why did they make the site? What is the site meant to give to people who visit it? Not every website is made to be a good source of information. Often, knowing who made the website and why can help you decide if the site is a good source of information or not.
2. When was the website made? When was it last updated? Is the information you're reading on the website new or old? Finding out when the information you're reading was posted can help you tell if you might be able to find newer information on other sites. Things may have changed since the old information was posted online.

3. Is the website easy to use? Can you easily find things you're looking for by searching the website?
4. Can you find information on this website on other websites? Is it just copying and posting information from other sources? Is there information on this website you couldn't find in a book?

Learn Even More

IN BOOKS

Greenhaven Press (Editor). *Nicki Minaj (People in the News)*. Farmington Hills, Mich.: Lucent Books, 2013.

Hill, Laban Carrick. *When the Beat Was Born: DJ Kool Herc and the Creation of Hip Hop*. New York: Roaring Brook Press, 2013.

Saddleback Educational Publishing. *Lil Wayne (Hip-Hop Biographies)*. St. Louis, Mo.: Turtleback Publishing, 2013.

Llanas, Sheila Griffin. *Hip-Hop Stars (Hip-Hop World)*. North Mankato, Minn.: Capstone Press, 2010.

ONLINE

Nicki Daily: Nicki Minaj Fan Website
www.nickidaily.com

Nicki's Official Website
www.mypinkfriday.com

Nicki Minaj on AllMusic
www.allmusic.com/artist/nicki-minaj-mn0001013175

Nicki Minaj on Billboard.com
www.billboard.com/artist/312259/nicki-minaj

Nicki Minaj on MTV.com
www.mtv.com/artists/nicki-minaj

Index

American Idol 31–33

Barbies 39
Beam Me Up Scotty 18–19, 22
Billboard 21–23, 29, 39, 45
business 9, 18, 20, 24, 37–39

Carey, Mariah 21, 31, 33
Come Up DVD, The 21
commercials 38

DeGeneres, Ellen 23
Dirty Money Records 18
Drake 19, 21, 23, 27
Dr. Dre 38

Eminem 23
fashion 37
father 9, 11–12

Fendi 18
Fox 32

Grammys 7–9, 25, 27

high school 13, 39

hip-hop 9, 14, 21–22, 25, 28–29, 38, 41

Ice Age: Continental Drift 39
Interview Magazine 21, 41
Internet 17, 19, 24

Jay-Z 21–22

Lil Wayne 19–20, 25

Mack Maine 22
Maine, Mack 22
Maraj, Carol 9
Minaj, Nicki (Onika Maraj) 7–8, 23, 29, 31, 34, 38–39, 41

mixtapes 18–19, 22
"Monster" 21
mother 9–12
MySpace 17–18

New York 10–11, 13, 38

Other Woman, The 39

Pink Friday 8, 20, 22–23, 27, 29, 38
Pink Friday: Roman Reloaded 27, 29
Playtime Is Over 18
pop 5, 23, 27–29, 31, 38, 41
Port of Spain 9

Randy, Jackson 31
rap 8, 13–14, 17, 19, 21, 23, 27–29, 39
Rihanna 23
Roman 7–8, 23, 27, 29, 41

social media 8, 17, 35, 41
St. James 9–10
"Starships" 39, 38
Sucka Free 18

"Super Bass" 23, 29
Swift, Taylor 23

Target 38
Teen Vogue 12–13, 21, 39, 41
Trachtenberg, Michelle 23
Trinidad and Tobago 9–10, 25
Twitter 8, 19, 31–32, 34–35

Vibe Magazine 23

We Are Young Money 21

Young Money Entertainment 21

Walmart 38
West, Kanye 21–22

About the Author

C.F. Earl is a writer living and working in Binghamton, New York. Earl writes on a range of topics, including pop culture, history, and health.

Picture Credits

Dreamstime.com:
    Carrienelson1: pp. 20, 32, 33
    Featureflash: pp. 6, 26, 36

Sbukley: pp. 16, 28, 30, 40
Serban Enache: p. 10

www.ingramcontent.com/pod-product-compliance
Lightning Source LLC
Chambersburg PA
CBHW041307110426
42743CB00037B/31